PRINCESS

JANINE KUBALA

PRINCESS

PRINCESS BY JANINE KUBALA

Published by Janine Kubala July 2008
Kubala Ministries
www.kubalaministries.org
info@kubalaministries.org
ABN: 15 129 631 876

Cover Design and Layout by Q Brand Agency

PRINCESS

National Library of Australia Cataloguing-in-Publication entry:
Author: Kubala, Janine.
Title: Princess: become everything you've been created to be / Janine Kubala.
ISBN: 9780980502800 (hbk.)
Notes: Bibliography.
Subjects: Women-Life skills guides, Women-Psychology.
Dewey Number: 646.70082.

FOR ANDREW

'I HAVE A DREAM

THAT ONE DAY EVERY VALLEY SHALL BE EXALTED,

AND EVERY HILL AND MOUNTAIN SHALL BE MADE LOW,

THE ROUGH PLACES WILL BE MADE PLAIN,

AND THE CROOKED PLACES WILL BE MADE STRAIGHT,

AND THE GLORY OF THE LORD SHALL BE REVEALED

AND ALL FLESH SHALL SEE IT TOGETHER.'

Martin Luther King, Jnr
Lincoln Memorial, Washington DC
28 August 1963

PRINCESS

'in the image and
likeness of God He
created him; male and
female He created them.'

PRINCESS

'AND God said, Let Us make mankind
in Our image, and after Our likeness;
And let them have complete authority over
the fish of the sea, the birds of the air, the
beasts, and over all of the earth, and over
everything that creeps upon the earth.
So God created man in His own image,
in the image and likeness of God He
created him; male and female He created
them. And God blessed them and said to
them, Be fruitful, multiply, and fill the earth,
and subdue it (using all of its vast resources
in the service of God and of man).'
GENESIS 1:26 -28

PRINCESS

'To see ourselves the way God sees us is like drawing back the curtains to reveal an unending scene of potential and destiny.'

PRINCESS

THE WOMAN I SEE

She is
Yielded;
Pure of heart;
Beautiful in presence and in form;
Her head is lifted as she stands to her full height,
strong and tall;
Looking forward, she smiles at what she sees;
The woman I see is magnificent.
The woman I see is you.

PRINCESS

'Our Father in heaven,
Hallowed be Your name.'

Matthew 6:9

PRINCESS

When I see women in our cities, out in the dark and cold, wearing close to nothing, selling themselves for just a couple of dollars, my heart breaks and I think,

'Princess, don't you know who you are?'

When I read in magazines and newspapers about women who are starving themselves, committing a slow and miserable form of suicide, my heart breaks and I think,

'Princess, don't you know who you are?'

When I see beautiful women trying to disguise their beauty and soothe their lonely, aching hearts with food, my heart breaks and I think,

'Princess, don't you know who you are?'

When I hear about women cutting and hurting themselves, trying to somehow balance the pain that overwhelms them on the inside, my heart breaks and I think,

'Sweet Princess, don't you know who you are?'

PRINCESS

THANK YOUS

This book would not have been possible without the unfailing support and encouragement of my husband Andrew. Thank you for loving me and for seeing things in me that I never knew were there.

My princes, Sam and Jonny. You are my gifts from God and my answered prayer. I love you and I am so proud of who you are becoming.

My parents, Alan and Valerie Grey, thank you for speaking life and destiny into my spirit and for loving me unconditionally.

My sisters Linda, Julie, Leanne and Alana, it is an honour to run this race alongside you.

To my 'other sister' Sharon Bohane. Thank you for being 'the real thing' and for encouraging me along this journey.

Susan Elijas, thank you for believing in the vision of this book, and for the many hours of proofreading and editing. You are lovely inside and out.

Phillip Sunderland and the team at Q Brand Agency, thank you for bringing the dream to life.

PRINCESS

Murray Thom, I am very grateful for your words of encouragement and wisdom, and for your timely advice. Thank you.

The Moody and Tulloch families, thank you for opening your homes to me and giving me the space to write in the most inspirational place in the world.

And to all of the amazing women whose photos appear in this book, you have given a name and a face to the word 'beautiful' and shown me what true beauty is all about.

Janine

'We are children of God. And if we are His children, then we are His heirs also; heirs of God and fellow heirs with Christ.' Romans 8:16-17

PRINCESS

CONTENTS

Post Card

FOR ADDRESS ONLY

THIS SPACE MAY BE USED FOR CORRESPONDENCE.

'You are a chosen race, a royal priesthood, a dedicated nation, God's own purchased, special people.'

1 Peter 2:9

PRINCESS

THE POWER OF A NAME

There are moments in life, through simple day-to-day conversations, when a word spoken often unknowingly, reveals a truth that resonates deeply within our spirits and in that moment time stands still as our vision is clarified, and the power of that truth marks us forever.

I remember one such moment. It happened during Christmas a few years ago. My husband and I were holidaying with my sister and her family in Perth. Soaking in the warmth of the Australian sunshine and watching my niece and nephew swim in the pool, my sister and I began to reminise about our childhood. We remembered our own poolside adventures and the summers which, back in those days, seemed to last forever.

I have four sisters and we have shared many adventures. All five of us were born close together in age, particularly us 'older three girls' as my two older sisters and I were often referred to. We have wonderful parents and they worked hard to make sure we were all treated exactly the same. I have discovered that fairness is paramount in large families, because even the slightest whiff of 'special treatment' will be met with outrage and violent protest by all other siblings, and so my parents did their best to make sure there were no favourites. We each had our own special name our parents called us by, and mine just happened to be 'Princess'. Princess Neanie to be precise.

As we talked and remembered it wasn't long before our conversation turned to the early years of our childhood which were impacted by my father's illness. In the early 1970's when eating disorders were barely even recognised amongst women, my father fought a battle with anorexia nervosa and depression, and attempted to take his own life on a number of occasions. This meant my sisters and I spent significant periods of time staying with family and friends, and because my father was unable to work; money was always tight.

We each had our own special name our parents called us by, and mine just happened to be 'Princess' …

In our conversation, when my sister recalled various events from our childhood, her memories were clouded with bitterness caused by the abandonment and embarrassment she had felt, and that had left her feeling like she was somehow less than everyone else. There are only 15 months that separate my sister and I in age, and as she spoke, even though I recalled all of the same events, my feelings associated with those memories were completely different. The memories I have of my childhood are happy ones. I always felt loved and secure and I never once doubted I was special. When I said to her, 'I do remember those things, I just don't remember them like that,' she looked at me and said, 'That's because you were the Princess.'

'Princess.' That was the word and it was also the moment of clarity that marked me forever. What was it about that word that had made such an impact and resulted in the incredible difference in the way my sister and I perceived ourselves and our lives? Somehow, instinctively I knew what it was. The word 'Princess' spoken continually throughout my childhood was an affirmation of my identity, and although I had never taken the time to consciously consider it before, I knew I had stumbled upon a profound truth. The power of a name.

The Bible tells us clearly and on a number of occasions who we are and what our name is. We are God's children, His heirs, and therefore 'Royalty.' Over and over again we are told we are 'a royal race,' 'a royal priesthood,' and that 'as kings we shall reign over the earth.' The royal lineage of mankind is undeniable and firmly established in God's word.

So, Princess, if this is who we really are, then why is it so difficult for us to get our heads, our hearts and our tongues around? Maybe you're thinking: what's the big deal, what does it matter anyway? In 'Romeo and Juliet' Shakespeare famously wrote 'What's in a name? That which we call a rose by any other name would smell as sweet.' But I have to disagree with Shakespeare on this one. There is so much in a name. Names are important because they are so powerful.

The international children's organisation UNICEF has stated that, 'the right to a name is the most fundamental of all human rights.'

'And You have made them a kingdom, a royal race, and priests to our God, and they shall reign as kings over the earth.' Revelation 5:10

In Matthew 6, when Jesus teaches the crowds how to pray He challenges them not to be misguided or hypocritical in the way they relate to God, but instead to approach Him in this manner, 'Our Father Who is in heaven, hallowed be Your name.' The foundational truth at the core of our identity is a recognition that we are children of the most hallowed being in the universe, and it is only once this identity has been established that we are able to relate to God with the boldness and the intimacy He desires, and proceed further into His purpose.

'Princess.' That is our name and it is our title. It is also the calling upon each one of our lives. We belong to God and He has given us value, authority, destiny and an inheritance. When we know who we are, when we really start to get it, then we no longer need permission to be extraordinary and we no longer need the approval of other people to do something great with our lives.

There is a woman in the Bible whose life I believe encapsulates the identity, the call and the power of women. She was a

Princess, a Queen in fact, and a woman of great courage and faith. She was a woman who knew who she was and what she was called to do. Most importantly, she was a woman who chose to surrender her own life to God's cause.

The woman I'm talking about is Esther. An orphan born into an enslaved and despised race, yet her humble beginnings were no barrier to the tremendous purpose God had for her life. When Esther stepped out of obscurity and into the spotlight of the Persian throne room she rose to all of the challenges put before her 'for such a time as this,' and through her courage she set in motion the course of events that shifted the balance of power in the Persian court and brought salvation to her people.

Just like most of us, Esther was not born into a royal household in an earthly sense with great wealth, privilege and status. Instead the position of 'Princess' was a calling she had to choose to accept and step into so that she could take hold of her destiny.

Esther may have been elevated to the position of Queen on earth, but that identity was not the source of her authority and in the end her earthly position could offer her no real protection. It is only when Mordecai reminds Esther of the lineage of her father's house and the absolute authority of her God that she makes the courageous decision to overcome her fears and step into the purpose God has for her life. Princess, each one of us has this same revelation to take hold of so that we too can live out our own incredible purpose.

'Do not flatter yourself that you shall escape in the king's palace any more than all the other Jews. For if you keep silent at this time relief and deliverance shall arise for the Jews from elsewhere, but you and your father's house will perish.' Esther 4:13-14

In this book we will journey together through the life of Esther and explore the four themes which were the hallmarks of her life; Beauty, Influence, Alignment and Authority. Each one of these themes form an essential part of our identity as women and reveal powerful keys that will unlock the potential and the destiny God has placed inside you. *Princess, as you read on, allow the Spirit of God to speak to your heart.*

[1] UNICEF Report, 'The Convention on the Rights of The Child', The Progress of Nations Summit 1996

PRINCESS

'The maiden was beautiful and lovely' *Esther 2:7*

BEAUTY

The one thing that Esther is most famous for is her beauty and it was her beauty that captured the attention of those around her and took her to the palace of the king.

Since the beginning of time the beauty of women has captured the attention and the hearts of men. Throughout history female beauty has been shown to be a captivating and powerful force so strong that it has started wars, divided families, and launched ships in their thousands.

There is no denying the power of a woman's beauty. You have probably noticed how often the image of a beautiful woman is used in advertising everything from floor tiles through to sports cars and pet food. I remember as a small child going into a mechanics workshop with my Dad and seeing a poster on the wall of beautiful woman. She was extremely voluptuous and wearing a very small bikini. That poster was advertising motor oil. I remember wondering, 'What on earth does that pretty lady have to do with oil?' Something that I have come to realise is that, as a general rule, gorgeous women and motor oil actually don't have that much in common. But what advertisers know very well is that the image of a woman will capture your attention more than any other image. More than the image of a good looking man, a cute baby, a beautiful sunset or a sleek sports car. What advertisers also know is that once your attention has been captured, the image of a woman will hold your attention for 30% longer than any other image, and it actually doesn't matter who is doing the looking, whether the person is male or female, adult or a child. The human response to the image of a woman is always the same.[2]

When we think about this in the context of the creation of women, it actually makes a whole lot of sense. Genesis 2:18 tells us that when God created Adam He said it was not good for him to be alone, and so He searched the whole earth looking for a suitable companion for Adam but found none. So God caused Adam to fall into a deep sleep and while he was sleeping God searched Adam's heart for just what it was that he desired above all else.

female beauty has been shown to be a captivating and powerful force so strong that it has started wars, divided families, and launched ships in their thousands.

Think about it. At this point God could have made anything or anyone to fulfil Adam's heart's desire. He could have made a sports car, a yacht, or a big leather lazy boy chair set up in front of a huge flat screen TV with every remote imaginable placed on the arm rest and a well-stocked fridge strategically located within arm's reach. But He didn't. I can almost hear the frustrated cries of men all around the world screaming out: 'Why on earth not? Why, God, why?'

Because when God searched Adam's heart for his most intimate desire and for what it was that would fulfil him the most, what did He find? Who did He see? Who did He make? He made you! As women we are the living embodiment of the heart's desire of man. Unlike Adam who was created from the earth, God created women from Adam's own flesh. Could it be that we are perhaps a more refined and sophisticated version of God's original design?

The truth about women is that not only have we been created in the image of God and called His daughters, we have also been created to be beautiful and desirable. It doesn't matter what our skin colour or body shape are, or whether our hair is long or short, straight or curly. It is not something we have to strive for or have plastic surgery to achieve. This beauty is an essential part of our feminine identity.

Princess, beauty is not the sum total of who we are as women, and it is certainly not the place where God wants all of our attention to be focused. However, as we will see from the life of Esther, our beauty must be respected and valued because it is the recognition of this beauty that is the starting point in discovering who God made when He created us.

---

[2] Gresh, D. 'Secret Keeper, The Delicate Power of Modesty', Moody Press Chicago 2002

PRINCESS

Kirrily

And her traffic stopping smile.

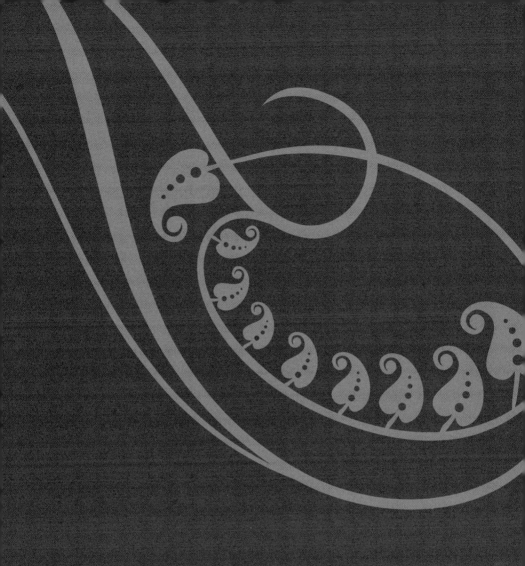

'THERE IS NOTHING
MORE BEAUTIFUL THAN
THE SMILE OF A FRIEND.'

'King Xerxes earnestly remembered Vashti (and so) the king's servants who ministered to him said, let beautiful young virgins be sought for the king... and let the maiden who pleases the king be made queen... This pleased the king, and he did so.' Esther 2:1-4

PRINCESS

HER BEAUTY
IS AUTHENTIC

This is where the journey begins for Esther. Just like in the story of Adam and Eve, it all starts with an 'earnest' longing in the heart of a man. You see, after divorcing his first wife, Vashti, Xerxes the Persian king, despite all of his great power and wealth, was unhappy. What his heart earnestly desired was a wife, someone to come alongside and support him. So a search was undertaken for the most beautiful young women in the kingdom to be brought before the king so that he could satisfy the longing in his heart and find a bride. His queen.

Inside the heart of every man exists a longing that can only be satisfied by female companionship and by the beauty that women possess. Now we are not talking about the popular versions of beauty that are created by trends and influenced by culture and time periods. I'm sure what was considered to be great beauty in ancient Persia would be considerably different to the perception of beauty in our current Western society. Even within the limits of our Western culture, think about how greatly the perception of beauty has changed over the past couple of generations. The busty and voluptuous form of Marilyn Monroe in the 1960s gave way to the doe-eyed girlishness of Twiggy in the 1970s. If you are a child of the '80s like me, then you won't have forgotten the reign of the 'Glamazons,' those statuesque supermodels who ruled the world from the 1980s to the early 1990s, refusing to get out of bed for anything less than $10,000 a day. As the turn of the century neared, it was the petite and pouty waifs of 'heroin chic' who turned the fashion world on its head. It's exhausting to even think about, let alone try to keep transforming ourselves to fit in with these ever-changing standards of female perfection.

I'm sure what was considered to be great beauty in ancient Persia would be considerably different to the perception of beauty in our current Western society.

I remember when, as a student at the University of Miami in Florida, hanging out at South Beach surrounded by the toned and tanned bodies of fellow beachgoers, I was astounded to hear my friend (a fellow international student from Bolivia) complain that he thought North American women were too perfect and plastic-looking, and that their perfectly waxed and manicured bodies made them look like 'plucked chickens.' His own personal preference was for women who had a bit more flesh and who valued every strand of their body hair. The comments of my Bolivian friend really caught my attention because he wasn't a weirdo, he was an intelligent, charming and very good looking young man. And yes, I did stop shaving my legs for a while.

But what I realised is that our perceptions of beauty are always so very different. Notions of popular beauty really do lie in the eye of the beholder. The truth is that there is no point in being distracted and discouraged by phases and trends or chasing after ideals of physical perfection that simply do not exist. They are moving targets. What is seen through the eyes of one person as being the physical embodiment of perfection will be seen through the eyes of another as a 'plucked chicken.'

The beauty that God made when he created women is an authentic form of beauty that is not derived from external appearance but instead flows from the centre of the feminine heart. Esther may have been considered a great beauty in her time but if physical beauty was the only thing she had going for her, then the harem and the walls of the palace would have soon become her prison. In the same way, the pursuit of outward beauty on its own will soon entrap and enslave us.

Esther's journey started with her physical beauty but her outward appearance was just the start of the qualities that made her beautiful. Above all else, what King Xerxes earnestly desired was someone with whom he could share his life. As women, it is our ability to come alongside to strengthen and support, and to bring improvement to life in every way that form the foundations of the authentic beauty that is an essential part of our identity. *Princess, it is these same qualities that must remain our focus.*

PRINCESS

My mother
Valerie

Her beauty has always taken my breath away.

'HER CHILDREN RISE UP
AND CALL HER BLESSED;
AND HER HUSBAND BOASTS
OF AND PRAISES HER.'

Proverbs 31:28

PRINCESS

'Now when the turn of each maiden came to go in to King Xerxes after the regulations for the women had been carried out for twelve months – since this was the regular period for their beauty treatments, six months with oil of myrrh and six months with sweetspices and perfumes and the things for the purifying of the women.' Esther 2:12

HER BEAUTY
MUST BE VALUED

Esther hit the jackpot! She got to spend one whole year in a spa. Can you imagine it? One year of beauty treatments, massages, facials and pedicures, with nothing to do but relax and be pampered. Sounds like heaven on earth to me.

Even though it may seem like an indulgence, and maybe a whole year of spa treatments is taking things a bit far, there is such power in nurturing our beauty because this is the very area that Satan targets most in women. Satan is a liar. He takes the truth, the beauty that God created when he made women, and he distorts and turns it around so that our thoughts become the opposite of truth. Thoughts like, 'I'm so ugly,' 'I'm so fat,' 'Nobody will ever love or desire me.'

Beauty and desirability form a foundational part of our feminine identity yet most of us spend our lives battling the feeling of ugly. The feeling that we are not quite pretty enough and are always one or two dress sizes away from that ideal weight. It may be triggered by different things in each one of us and hard to define precisely, but the feeling of ugly is something that affects us all. If you have ever had one of those days when a bad hair day and a fat day coincide, then you will know exactly what I am talking about. The feeling of ugly tells us that we are worthless and that we'll never be good enough. It isolates us and makes us feel like we are the only ones who don't quite have it all together.

I have wasted such a huge part of my life being dissatisfied and critical of my body. When I was younger I despised my body so completely that just the sight of my own image reflected in a window or mirror would immediately cause me to start cursing and swearing at the image I saw before me. In my eyes, my body was disgusting and whenever I looked at myself, I only ever saw my faults. The greatest battle of my life so far has been overcoming the depression and eating disorders that controlled my life for almost a decade.

One of the symptoms of my disease was a refusal to make much of an effort with my appearance. I often wore oversized men's clothing and I had no time for make-up or manicures because I was determined not to become 'one of those superficial, phony girls.' Whenever my mother challenged me to make more of an effort with my appearance I would always justify myself by saying, 'People should accept me the way I am, and if they don't then they are the ones with the problem!' However, the truth was that deep down underneath all of my excuses and pious justifications, I despised myself and I could see no point in wasting time and money investing care into something I believed had no value: me.

The heart's cry of every woman is for an affirmation of her value and for me, recognising the power of caring for and valuing myself not only transformed my thinking but it also bought healing to my life. I have come to realise that I don't need to care for my appearance to give me value, but instead I need to care for myself because of my value, and so, to combat Satan's attacks against our identity we must choose to live out the truth by treating ourselves in a way that is consistent with God's word. This is where the spa treatments come in.

'And you will know the Truth and the Truth will make you free.' John 8:32

For me one of the most powerful breakthroughs I have made in dealing with a very negative body image was when I made a conscious effort to start treating myself with kindness and respect. Now whenever I feel my mind starting to go down that pathway of self-criticism, I stop and thank God for my body which is 'wonderful and fearfully made' and then take a moment to show some kindness to the body that serves me so well, even if it is just taking a few seconds to tidy my hair. Something that I love to do is to run a bath and have a long soak, put treatments in my hair and do my nails. What I have discovered is that it is very hard to despise yourself when you have just been so kind to yourself.

As women there will always be something else to do and someone else's needs to meet. This isn't something we should complain about or become resentful over, we just need to recognise that in the midst of our unrelenting schedules we need to take time to love, pamper and care for ourselves. I don't say this in the context of making our appearance an idol or an obsession, but rather in the context of loving and caring for ourselves in the way God intended us to.

God's word tells us that our bodies are temples of His Spirit and that He intended for them to serve us and to be a blessing to us during our life on earth. When we think about our bodies in this way it just doesn't make any sense for us to starve, abuse or neglect them.

'Do you not know that your body is the temple of the Holy Spirit Who lives within you, Whom you have from God? You are not your own?' 1 Corinthians 6:19

It is so interesting that out of all of the preparations Esther could have undertaken for the greatest role of her life, so much of her time and energy was invested into developing and enhancing her beauty. This investment was not the result of vanity, it was simply obedience to the authority God had placed over her, and it was this investment into her beauty that led Esther further along the journey of God's purpose for her life. Concern for our appearance should never be something that rules or drives us but we do need to invest time and care into developing our beauty because it affirms such a foundational part of our identity.

God made us beautiful. He made us desirable. Not by chance or coincidence but by intention and design. In a culture that is obsessed with youth and beauty the temptation can be to react against this by opting out all together. We need to be aware of how damaging this is to us as women. It is a violation of an essential part of our identity. *Princess, what better stand to take than to value and cherish our femininity and present ourselves beautifully and without pretence as a natural extension of who God created us to be.*

Georgia, Mila & Taylor

'THE SPLENDOUR of GOD
EXPRESSED THROUGH YOU
WILL BE REVEALED AS a
FORM of BEAUTY THAT is
EXCLUSIVELY YOURS.'

'Now when the turn for Esther had come, to go in to the king, she required nothing but what Hegai the king's attendant, the keeper of the women, suggested. And Esther won favour in the sight of all who saw her.'

Esther 2:15

HER BEAUTY IS UNIQUE

There was something special about Esther. Even though she was brought to the palace as part of a harem, just one of many beautiful women, she stood out. Esther was different and, as it happened, it was the very thing that made her different that also captured Hegai's attention and bought her favour.

When God created us He didn't use carbon paper. Instead He harnessed all of His creative genius to form every person as a different expression of His own image and likeness. We have been formed in the image and likeness of God, not everybody else, and the course our lives take will play out differently for each one of us. There is no one on the planet like you, with the exact same combination of passion, humour, intellect, and style. There never has been and there never again will be. You are unique, and the splendour of God expressed through you will be revealed as a form of beauty that is exclusively yours.

The 'beauty pageant' factor in the story of Esther brings back to me so clearly the scenes from my own experience in the world of modelling as a teenager. From the backstage chaos at fashion shows to the early morning craziness in preparation for a photo shoot, there was always an endless array of cosmetics, clothes, shoes, and accessories all shrouded in a heavy mist of hairspray. Then of course there were the other women or 'girls' as we were always called, and the frenzy of activity as we readied ourselves for our moment to shine.

Just like within the walls of the harem, those backstage scenes had the potential to become a hotbed of insecurity and jealousy as we all checked each other out and sized up the competition. Like women all around the world we so often fell into the trap of comparing ourselves with each other to see who was the prettiest, the thinnest, who had the best outfits, and who was the new 'favourite' and had been booked to do the best jobs.

These characteristics may be more pronounced in the world of modelling but they are certainly not exclusive to it. This is a scenario that is played out in every schoolyard, university campus, office building and church around the world. One of the greatest battles we fight as women is against our own insecurity and the temptation to compare ourselves to others. Our beauty is a gift from God but so often that gift remains ignored and unappreciated as our eyes longingly covet the form of the gift God has given to someone else.

During my early twenties I spent a number of years working in Indonesia and I was constantly taken back by the extraordinary beauty of the women from this nation. The form of their beauty was delicate and petite, they had glossy raven hair, dark almond eyes and olive skin. I am by comparison six foot tall, broad shouldered and athletic in build. I have blue eyes and my fair skin refuses to tan no matter how much time I spend in the sun. In comparing myself to these women I always came away feeling like a heavy and cumbersome giant. That is the danger of comparison and it is one of the greatest crimes we can ever commit against ourselves. Whenever we compare ourselves to something we are not, we will always fall short because God never designed or intended for us to be anyone but ourselves. I will never be a delicate lotus blossom but that does not negate my own personal form of beauty.

It is impossible for us to relate to each other in a healthy way as women until we get the revelation for ourselves that God has made us unique and given us each our own personal brand of beauty and style. The truth is, so often it is the things that make us different that also make us beautiful.

'It is not good that the man should be alone; I will make him a helper meet (suitable, adapted, complementary) for him.' Genesis 2:18

The very purpose of Esther being placed in inside the harem with all those other women was so that she would be supported and cared for by them as she undertook her preparations to meet the king. It is interesting that it was for this same reason that God created Eve, the first woman, so that she would be a companion and helper for Adam. It is so important that we don't forget the original purpose of our creation. It is when we work together, not in competition, that we can help and complement each other.

It is not by coincidence that Esther's relationships with other women were established in such an intense and competitive environment. I believe God wanted to demonstrate that the insecurities and jealousy that plague us all can be overcome. *Princess, it is only when we choose to view our sisters and girlfriends as companions and allies instead of competitors that we will be free to realise the beauty that is uniquely ours.*

My sisters

Linda, Julie, Leanne, Janine & Alana

At war during our childhood over
clothes and shoes, now we are
grown we are each others greatest
supporters and closest allies.

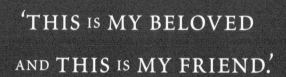

'THIS IS MY BELOVED
AND THIS IS MY FRIEND.'

Song of Solomon 5:16
New King James Version

'So, when the king's command and decree were proclaimed, and when many maidens were gathered at Shushan the capital, under the custody of Hegai, Esther also was taken to the king's house, into the custody of Hegai, the keeper of the women.' *Esther 2:8*

SHE VALUES THE BEAUTY
OF HER FRIENDSHIPS
WITH WOMEN

Esther spent one year exclusively in the care and company of other women as she prepared to be brought into the presence of King Xerxes for the first time. Can you imagine the scene as 400 women and their attendants prepared and readied themselves for their turn at trying to win the love and affection of one man?[3]

I am sure the intensity of the competition involved brought out the dark side of women that we all possess. Can you imagine the gossip and backstabbing as jealousies and insecurities ran rampant in such an extreme setting? My initial reaction when I imagined this scene was that it would truly be one of my worst nightmares. But as I considered things further I had the revelation that this scene is actually a powerful indication of the value of our time with our sisters and girlfriends.

I love watching young girls together, playing and laughing; it seems impossible for them not to be affectionate with each other. I have witnessed this beautiful female characteristic in so many settings and it seems that whenever young girls get together there will always be constant embracing, hand holding, and hair doing.

What about female conversations? As women, we have the ability to get to the heart of the matter very quickly and even the briefest of conversations can be filled with continuous encouragements and affirmations. You look gorgeous. I love your hair, your outfit, and of course, your shoes! How many times have you unsuspectingly entered a ladies' bathroom only to stumble upon an 'encouragement intervention' being staged by a group of girlfriends trying to soothe the heart and lift the spirits of one of their precious friends?

I love this about women. We intuitively seem to know what each other wants and needs. Whether it is a simple compliment and some affirmation, or a gentle touch that reminds us we are not alone, or maybe it's just some silliness and laughter that raises our spirits and causes our perspective to be lifted above our feelings and circumstances. It is no surprise then that Esther received the strength and the support she needed to undertake the greatest challenge of her life in the care and the company of other women, because it is through our friendships with other women that we ourselves are cared for.

The day after the arrival of our second son Jonathan, my husband had to travel overseas to work for a number of weeks. I thought that I would be fine; this was my second child and I had done it all before, so the second time around it would all be a piece of cake, right? I was so wrong! Within a couple of days of Andrew's departure, I was a complete wreck. Exhaustion has a way of making you crazy and I had entered the realms of complete insanity. In the midst of my turmoil I received a call from my friend Rachel, asking how I was and if I needed anything. Immediately my mind was filled with needs that were many and desperate. Sleep! Sanity! I need a clean house, clean laundry, some adult conversation and a hug from my mum. My needs were so overwhelming that they were impossible to articulate and, as is so often the case when we really do need help, my answer to her was, 'Nothing. I don't need anything. We are all doing great!'

As women, we have the ability to get to the heart of the matter very quickly and even the briefest of conversations can be filled with continuous encouragements and affirmations.

Thankfully, Rachel was able to see through my thinly veiled stoicism because Rachel is a woman and a mother of four young children herself. She refused to take 'No' for an answer and she said to me, 'Janine, I am going to make you dinner for the next week.' God bless Rachel! Who else but a woman could possibly know and understand the needs of another woman? When Rachel arrived to deliver her first meal, the first thing she said to me as she took my hands and looked into my eyes was this, 'Janine you are a fantastic mother.' More than anything else this was the area I needed to be reassured in because I felt like I was failing miserably. Somehow, Rachel knew exactly how to encourage me and speak into my life.

For the next week Rachel made me dinner, and we are not talking about a week's worth of tuna casserole to put in the freezer. Every evening Rachel came to my home with a delicious and beautifully prepared meal, and each afternoon I would eagerly watch the clock, counting down the time until her arrival, because even more than the nourishment of her meals, I looked forward to her company. Rachel was my link to sanity and a world beyond night feeds and nappies. She gave me good advice and she helped me get things into perspective. The behaviour of my three year old son that drove me to distraction throughout the day somehow became not such a big deal, and even funny, when I shared it with Rachel.

it is so important for us to learn how to manage and negotiate our friendships so that they last a lifetime…

Rachel saw me at my most vulnerable, exhausted and strung out, with messy hair, and mismatched clothes. Yet it was from this place of vulnerability that our friendship grew and was strengthened because it is only when we let our guard down and allow ourselves to be vulnerable that we can develop the intimacy and heart connections that truly join us together.

As women, we need each other. There is such great power in the connection and partnership of women living their lives together, running the race alongside each other, supporting, encouraging and cheering each other on. That is why it is so important for us to learn how to manage and negotiate our friendships so that they last a lifetime and are not stopped short by the 'dark side of women' that we all possess.

Our relationships with our sisters and girlfriends are precious and they must be treasured and invested into because it is through these relationships that we ourselves are loved, supported and cared for. Esther benefited from the close attention and company of other women as she prepared to undertake the greatest role of her life. *Princess, in the same way our own lives are strengthened and made so much better through the power of friendship.*

3 Charles Swindoll, 'Esther, A Woman of Dignity and Strength', Word Publishing 1997

'Mordecai gave him a copy of the decree to destroy them, that he might show it to Esther, explain it to her, and charge her to go to the king, make supplication to him, and plead with him for the lives of her people.'

Esther 4:8

INFLUENCE

It is interesting that in the book of Esther, a book that bears her name, Esther herself does not appear in either the opening or closing chapters, and neither does she appear in much of the action. It is Mordecai, her cousin and adopted parent, her husband King Xerxes, and Haman, the evil anti-Semite and the king's second-in-command, who take centre stage and who seem to possess much of the power. Yet even though Esther herself doesn't feature in much of the action, her presence is still felt strongly throughout the whole book and she plays her most significant and strategic role through the power of her influence.

'Now numerous Samaritans from that town believed in and trusted in Him because of what that woman said when she declared and testified.' John 4:39

In creating women as the desire of man's heart, God has entrusted women with an amazing and powerful gift: influence. This influence is demonstrated again and again throughout the Bible. We see it in the story of the Samaritan woman who, after she encounters Jesus at a well, influences her village to believe and trust in Him. We see it also at the tomb of Jesus when, on the third day, the resurrected Christ chooses to reveal himself first to a group of women. Why? Because there was a whole world that needed to be influenced.

The power of this influence is also seen in the story of Sampson and Delilah where Delilah uses her influence to expose Sampson's weakness to his enemies, and again in the life of King Solomon whom God warns not to marry foreign women because they will influence his heart away from Him and introduce their own gods. Solomon ignores God's warning and it is his downfall.[4 & 5]

The place where this influence is perhaps demonstrated most powerfully is in the Garden of Eden when Satan approaches Eve in order to get to Adam. Imagine the scene outlined in Genesis 3:6 when Adam is approached by his beautiful wife Eve who is completely naked and holding an apple. Eve says to him, 'Hey, Adam, take a bite of this,' and Adam says, 'Whatever you say, Baby!' The poor guy didn't stand a chance. If you're married, why don't you try it out? That's the way that I get my husband to eat all of his fruit and vegetables!

'She took of it's fruit and ate; and she gave some also to her husband, and he ate.' Genesis 3:6

The thing I find most fascinating about this verse is that Eve does not even have to try to convince Adam to eat the fruit.

She doesn't engage him in any discussion or debate, she simply presents him with the fruit and without even the smallest amount of resistance, Adam takes hold of what he knows is forbidden and eats, and the fate of mankind is sealed.

The influence that we have as women is profound, and we must not underestimate its power. As we have seen, that influence can be used for great good or it can be distorted and used to expose, manipulate and bring destruction.

When Esther makes the courageous decision to go before the king to intervene on behalf of her people, she uses her influence with courage, wisdom and remarkable restraint. *Princess, the use of our influence must be guided by these same characteristics.*

[4] Judges 16:15-19

[5] 1 Kings 11:1-3

PRINCESS

Maree

Changing the world!

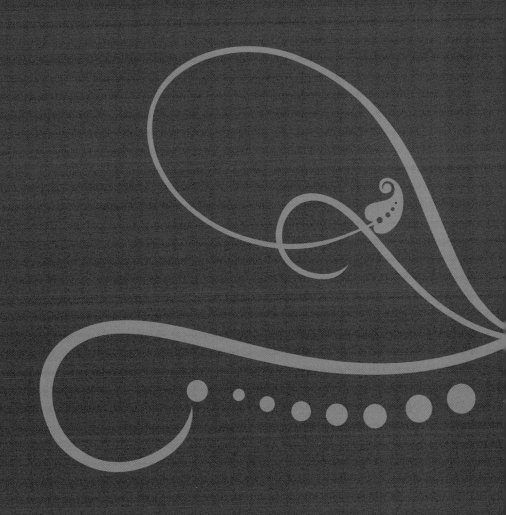

'COURAGE IS NOT THE
ABSENCE OF FEAR; IT IS
A DECISION TO STAND
AND ACT REGARDLESS.'

Author Unknown

'For if you keep silent at this time relief and deliverance shall arise for the Jews from elsewhere, but you and your father's house will perish.' *Esther 4:14*

SHE USES HER INFLUENCE
WITH COURAGE

As women we have been entrusted with the power of influence and we need to make use of it. It is God given. In the book of Esther that influence plays out like this: an irrevocable decree has been sent throughout the Persian Empire that legislates for the complete annihilation of the Jewish people. It specifies a date, a time and a method. Mordecai tells Esther to go before the king and to make supplication, to plead with him to do something to save the lives of her people. And then he speaks those famous words encouraging her to look beyond her fears and step into her destiny.

'And who knows but that you have come to the kingdom for such a time as this and for this very occasion.' Esther 4:14

It's easy to lose sight of the enormity of what Mordecai was asking Esther to do. Maybe, like me, you're thinking: 'What's the big deal? She's his wife. She's beautiful. All she has to do is put on a fetching outfit, use a bit of that influence, give the king a come hither look and she'll have him eating out of her hand like a little lamb.'

The reality though was quite different. Esther may have been the queen, but no one, queen or otherwise was free to walk into the king's presence and negotiate any decision that he made. This wasn't the palace lounge room where the king was casually hanging out watching a DVD. This was his war room where he discussed state business, made secret deals and discussed military strategy with a handful of trusted advisors. If the king was interested in speaking with anyone else then they had to be thoroughly screened beforehand. And let's face it, King Xerxes did not build the greatest empire on earth by being an old softy and a pushover.

It is such a challenge for us to consider just how many times we have been robbed of purpose and destiny by our fears and insecurities.

In order for Esther to have an audience with the king he had to send for her first, and at the time he hadn't sent for her in a month. If she went to him without first being summoned then she would be killed. It was the law. End of story. On top of all of that, Esther was Jewish, a fact that the king was not yet aware of, and as a gentile himself, who was to know how he would respond to that information?

There were so many reasons why it made no sense for Esther to do what Mordecai had asked of her. The risks were just way too high. And yet she pressed on regardless because in her discussion with Mordecai he had given her a revelation of her purpose and her destiny.

It is such a challenge for us to consider just how many times we have been robbed of purpose and destiny by our fears and insecurities. And on how many occasions has the destiny that God first intended for us been given to someone else to fulfil because we lacked the courage to take hold of it?

One of the greatest obstacles that I have had to overcome in choosing to make use of my influence has been my shyness. For a long time being shy was actually my trademark, and it was often the way that I was distinguished from my four other sisters. 'Janine? Oh, you mean the shy one.'

A couple of years ago God really started to challenge me about getting to know my neighbours. I had lived in my house for almost a year and I hadn't even seen my neighbours, let alone found out their names or anything about them. The great irony of all of this is that my husband and I run a ministry where our vision and stated goal is the salvation of our nation. And so God began to challenge me, 'Janine how can you influence your nation when you can't even influence your neighbours?' I had to admit that He made a good point.

You would think that God was asking me to walk through fire the way that I carried on. 'But God, what will I say to them? But God, you know that I stutter when I get nervous! But God, you know that I'm shy - it's not my fault, you made me this way!'

It got to the point where I could not even look at my neighbour's house without crying because I would think, 'What if they go through their whole lives and no one ever tells them about Jesus?' But still I lacked the courage to walk the twenty metres from my house to theirs, knock on the door and say, 'Hi, I'm your neighbour.'

In order for us to fulfil the destiny God has for each one of us, there will be moments in our journey where we must make the decision to simply obey God regardless of the cost or of how much it frightens us. Courage is not the absence of fear, it is a decision to stand and act regardless.[6]

influence is a gift God has freely given us, the decision to make use of this gift is one that only we can make…

So I took a deep breath and walked over to the house of my neighbour and knocked on her door. As I stood in the doorway rehearsing my lines and trying to compose myself I heard a voice scream at me from an upstairs window, 'Can you come back later, I'm really busy with the kids!' I felt absolutely relieved, yet completely let down all at the same time. But I had done it. I had faced my fear and going back the second time wasn't nearly as hard as it was the first.

OK, so the immediate result of my visit to my neighbour may appear to an outside observer to have been somewhat underwhelming. But for me it was a defining moment in my life. In taking that small step, I had actually crossed over an invisible line that signified my decision to choose obedience and purpose over fear and insecurity. I may be shy but I refuse to look back over my life with regret at what could have been because I allowed my fears to override my destiny.

God knew exactly what he was doing when He made us. And it is not by chance that we have been given the gift of influence. And while that influence is a gift God has freely given us, the decision to make use of this gift is one that only we can make.

Esther's decision not to remain silent but to make use of her influence and embrace the role for which she was born took both courage and a revelation of a higher purpose. *Princess, it is these same attributes embraced in our own lives that will enable us to step into our own incredible purpose.*

[6] Author Unknown

Bella

A face and a voice like an angel.

On our first date, Bella serenaded Andrew and I with a song he had written. It was during this song that I knew Andrew was the man I would marry.

'AND SHE SHALL BE CALLED WOMAN.'

Genesis 2:23

'On the seventh day, when the king's heart was merry with wine, …he commanded Queen Vashti (to come before him), with her royal crown, to show the peoples and the princes her beauty, for she was fair to behold. But Queen Vashti refused to come at the king's command.'

Esther 1:10 – 12

SHE UNDERSTANDS THE INFLUENCE OF HER WORDS

Queen Vashti said, 'No!' Can you believe it? If you are anything like me, this is the point where you stand up and start cheering for her. 'Good for you, Girlfriend! You stand up for yourself.' As women, we cheer Queen Vashti on as she takes a stand for women throughout her nation and opposes her tyrant husband. What kind of husband would want his own wife to become an object of lust and to be drooled over by his drunken party guests anyway? Someone needed to put Xerxes in his place!

Have you ever noticed how you can start out being so right but somehow end up being so wrong? I believe this is what happened for Queen Vashti. Although I don't necessarily disagree with her outrage at her husband's request, let's not forget that as well as being her husband he was also her king. I can't help but wonder whether things would have turned out very differently for her if she hadn't chosen to convey her disapproval in a manner that caused King Xerxes such huge public embarrassment and was such an affront to his position as king.

As women, the influence of our words is profound. It was because of the level of Vashti's influence that King Xerxes was counselled to divorce her. It was feared that through the influence of her words, Vashti would cause contempt for husbands to rise up in the hearts of women throughout the kingdom.

'For this deed of the Queen will become known to all women, making their husbands contemptible in their eyes, since they will say King Xerxes commanded Queen Vashti to be bought before him, but she did not come.'
Esther 1:17

I can almost hear the voice of my mother right now offering that often-quoted piece of advice: 'It is not just what you say, it's also how you say it that matters.' Surely, there could have been some other way for Queen Vashti to communicate her feelings to the king that would have served them both better and preserved their relationship.

It is so interesting to compare this with the way Queen Esther communicated her cause to the king. When Esther is accepted into the king's presence and given the opportunity to reveal her grievance to him, it is what she doesn't do that reveals so much about her character. She doesn't berate him and beat him up with her words; she doesn't break down sobbing and try to emotionally blackmail him with tears and tantrums; she doesn't try to manipulate him with seduction; and neither does she employ the use of guilt, deceptive words or unrelenting nagging to influence his heart toward her cause. She simply invites him to have dinner with her.

I believe one of the reasons Esther was able to exercise so much self control was because she was aware of both the power of her words and the power of her influence. Remember the story of the fall of man outlined in Genesis when Adam doesn't even need any convincing but simply accepts and takes hold of what Eve has presented to him?[7]

I remember when my husband and I first moved to Auckland to start our ministry, it was three hours of travelling to our closest family members, our son Samuel was five months old and we were just starting out in so many ways. Andrew was frequently away travelling and I was working full-time in our ministry, as well as caring for our son. One day Andrew innocently asked why I hadn't ironed his shirts. Little did he know the size of the beast that he was about to unleash. In hindsight I should have just taken it all as a big compliment because he obviously thought that I was superwoman.

But I was exhausted and I knew that my grievances were legitimate. I had been over them again and again in my mind. So I just let him have it and as I presented my case to him any truth it contained became completely distorted by my emotion, anger and resentment. 'You treat me like a slave. You don't love me, you don't care about me.' And I finished it all off with this: 'And you are not a good husband!' I have to admit that for a moment I did feel a whole lot better once I got that off my chest.

Not once throughout my tirade did my husband fight back or resist my words and I mistakenly read from his silence that he was ignoring me. So I let him have it again and again until he finally looked at me in complete defeat and said, 'You're right. I am not a good husband. I am obviously not capable of loving or caring for you in the way you need me to. It's clear that I'm not making you happy. And to be completely honest I am not happy either. I don't think that I can do this anymore.'

we must determine to either use that incredible influence to speak life into the people around us or keep our mouths firmly closed until we can…

At that moment I was on the brink of losing the relationship and the one person in my life who is the most precious to me. Under my influence he had taken on board the lies and the half truths I had presented to him. And under my influence he had taken my distorted perspective on board as his own. Just like Queen Vashti I stood to lose everything that mattered to me most because in the heat of the moment I lost sight of the power of my tongue and I spoke out words that, once they had been said, were impossible to take back.

I married a great man, who in our marriage has shown himself to be very patient and long-suffering, which as any member of my family will tell you, are the necessary requirements for a harmonious life with me! We were able to resolve our differences and recover from the destruction caused by my words. But what I am learning is that biting my tongue and remaining silent in the heat of the moment will save me a whole lot of grief and apologising later on.

What I love about Esther is that in the moment when she stood before the king, a moment in which there was so much at stake and in which she must have been so highly charged emotionally, she didn't just rush in and speak out of her emotion. Instead, she allowed herself to be disciplined by wisdom, and she took a step back from the issue that was causing her so much grief by extending a simple dinner invitation. In doing so she and the king were both able to benefit from a revelation of the bigger picture and in the events that unfolded Esther was able to communicate with absolute clarity what emotional words never could.

Princess, we hold the power of life and death in our tongues, and like Esther before us we must determine to either use that incredible influence to speak life into the people around us or to keep our mouths firmly closed until we can.

[7] Genesis 3:6

Mel

No matter how dark and cold the day may be, when Mel's around the sun always seems to be shining.

'YOU HAVE RAVISHED
MY HEART AND GIVEN
ME COURAGE WITH ONE
LOOK FROM YOUR EYES.'

Song of Solomon 4:9

'Go, gather together all the Jews that are present in Shushan, and fast for me; and neither eat nor drink for three days, night or day. I also and my maids will fast as you do.' Esther 4:16

SHE UNDERSTANDS THE INFLUENCE OF HER PRAYERS

Throughout the Bible fasting is employed as a method for seeking God and of using the time normally spent in the preparation and eating of meals, in prayer. Esther 4:16 not only gives us a powerful insight into Esther's character, it also reveals the secret of her success. I believe the greatest opportunity we have to exert our influence is through prayer. It was the power of prayer that Esther harnessed and held fast to as she undertook her impossible mission.

After meeting with Mordecai and accepting the mission to go before the king, Esther refused to do anything until she had first sought and waited on God. She was determined to hear from Him and to receive specific instruction as to how she should proceed before she took even one step. She knew that she needed His guidance.

There are only three days and one verse that separate Esther's decision to go before the king and the moment where we find her standing in the inner court of the king's throne room. And the Bible remains silent on the details of those three crucial days. But it was during the silence of those days as Esther waited on God that she received the courage and strength that enabled her to stand with confidence before the greatest kingdom on earth. It was also during that period of silent waiting that Esther allowed God to work in her heart and in the hearts of others.

In a message I heard recently, the pastor made a statement that really struck a chord with me and made me smile. He said, 'the only difference between a praying woman and a pit bull terrier is lipstick.'[8] Now that is a statement I know to be true. My mother is like a pit bull terrier in the best possible way. She prays and she keeps on praying and she won't give up or drop the matter even long after her lipstick has worn off.

In the early years of their marriage, my father and mother were saved at a Billy Graham crusade. I remember my mum telling me that in the moments after her salvation, when she stood in awe and in absolute gratitude to God for what He had done in her life, she started to cry out to Him, 'God, My life is yours, whatever you want me to do, I will do it for you.' She said that God spoke to her very clearly and said, 'I want your children.' And so that has been the mission my mother has devoted her life to, raising her children to not only know about God but to devote their lives to serving His cause. It is a mission she has taken very seriously and about which she has enormous passion. From before I was born and to this very moment I know that my mother has been and is praying for me.

There was a time in my life when for a number of years I walked away from God and shut my family out. I gave my parents no authority to speak into my life and they had to stand back and watch in silence as I traveled down pathways that could only lead to death and destruction. My life was controlled by eating disorders and depression and, in the eyes of many, I was a lost cause. I was hopelessly lost.

I felt darkness like an ice cold sword enter my heart. But without even thinking I woke myself up screaming out the name of Jesus.

Thankfully, my mum didn't give up on me and even though she lacked the ability to speak into my life, she never once stopped praying for me. I recall in one of my blackest moments having a dream where I was having a conversation with Satan. In our chat, Satan told me that it was within his power to give me everything I wanted, wealth, success in my career and that he was more than happy for me to keep my eating disorder so I would never be fat. All I had to do was live for him. Satan had nailed the desires of my heart, and right off the bat! My top three! So my reply was, 'Sold! Where do I sign?'

Immediately I felt darkness like an ice cold sword enter my heart. But without even thinking I woke myself up screaming out the name of Jesus. I got out of my bed and on my knees and I prayed, asking Jesus to forgive me, to come and live in my heart and to restore my relationship with God. It was 3.07am when I prayed that prayer. I then got back into bed and slept like a baby until morning, in complete peace.

My mum later told me that at 3.00am on that same morning, in a different city hundreds of kilometres away, God had woken her up and told her that she needed to pray for me, and so she did. From 3.00am until sunrise she cried out to God on my behalf. There is no doubt in my mind that the reason that I am alive and a Christian today is because of the prayers of my mother. The moment Satan had intended for my destruction became the moment of my salvation because of the power of one woman's prayers.

The power of prayer is what Esther took hold of to turn that impossible situation around in the Persian Empire all of those years ago. *Princess, it is this same power that we must also take hold of if we want to see hearts changed and nations transformed. And speaking as someone who was 'a hopeless cause' and whose life has now been transformed, I hope we will never lose sight of the powerful influence of our prayers.*

---

[8] Ps Leon Fontaine, Pursuit of Excellence Conference, Auckland, New Zealand, May 2005

PRINCESS

My Grandma Margaret

We share the same hands and the same heart but sadly not the same singing voice.

'SHE IS CLOTHED WITH

STRENGTH AND DIGNITY,

SHE CAN LAUGH AT THE

DAYS TO COME'

Proverbs 31:25
New International Version

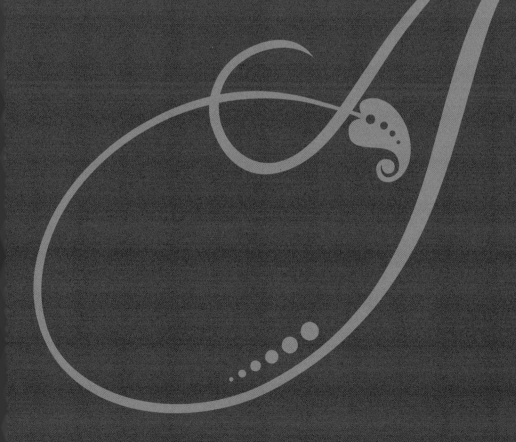

'And the command of Esther confirmed these observances of Purim, and it was written in the book.' *Esther 9:32*

SHE USES HER INFLUENCE TO INSPIRE THE GENERATIONS

Esther's last recorded act and perhaps her most enduring legacy was in establishing the Festival of Purim which commemorates God's remarkable deliverance of the Jewish people. The name of the festival comes from the word 'Pur' which means 'to cast lots' because it was by the casting of lots that Haman had determined the day on which he intended to destroy the Jewish people.[9] But as things turned out, this was the very day that the Jewish people experienced their greatest victory and the sovereignty of God was displayed throughout the kingdom. I love the way the word of God puts it. In Esther 9:1 in classic Biblical understatement, it says this:

'And so it was that on the very day that the enemies of the Jews had planned for a massacre of them, it was turned to the contrary and the Jews had rule over those who hated them.'

Now that is a moment worth remembering and celebrating.

Every family needs traditions; they are what create a sense of belonging and they are at the heart of what family is all about. In my family it was my mum who did most of the work involved in bringing everyone together and in making those occasions special. Christmas especially was always a big deal and even now, many years after my childhood I can tell you exactly what Christmas was like in our house.

Christmas Eve would begin with the long walks Mum would always make us take to visit neighbours and look for signs of reindeer. Or was it just to wear us all out? Then, huge excitement the next morning as five screaming girls ran into the lounge room where our Santa sacks, carefully laid out the night before, were now all overflowing with bounty from Mattel. Next, into the dining room for a family breakfast. This was the biggest deal of all, because this was the one time of the year when my very health-conscious father allowed us to eat commercial breakfast cereal. Every year Mum would buy a variety pack of Kellogg's finest, and we all got to choose and write our names on our own little box. And let me tell you, after a year of unsweetened porridge with wheat germ, a packet of Rice Bubbles never tasted so good. Finally, we would all head off to church, all five girls wearing varying shades of the same outfit and tightly clutching our new favourite toy.

It amazes me how all of these years later just the sight of a tiny box of Rice Bubbles brings back such strong feelings of comfort, love and belonging. But that is the power of our memories.

The intention of the Festival of Purim is clearly laid out. It was to be celebrated so the victories of the Jewish people on that day would be remembered forever and 'imprinted on the minds of every generation.' I love that. It seems to come so much more naturally for us to remember our defeats and the things that went wrong. It is only with purposeful intention that our victories will be celebrated, imprinted on our minds and remembered for generations to come.

'These days should be remembered (imprinted on their minds) and kept throughout every generation in every family, province, and city, and these days of Purim should never cease from among the Jews, nor the commemoration of them cease among their descendants.'

Esther 9:28

In our families and in our churches it is so important that we take the time to celebrate and remember our victories, establishing our own 'Festivals of Purim' so that there is not one generation who misses out on hearing about the goodness of God, His faithfulness and His sovereignty. In choosing to remember we enable the power of past victories to live on.

I never met my Grandma, my mum's mother. She died a few weeks before my birth. But I have always felt such a strong connection to her and, even though we didn't live on the earth at the same time, I feel like I know her and that she has played a huge role in making me who I am.

Some of my earliest memories are of sitting on my mum's knee and hearing her talk about my Grandma. She told me what an incredible woman Grandma was and how she was loved by everyone in the neighborhood because she was a great friend and someone who was always ready to help out in a crisis. She told me that Grandma was a straight talker who didn't suffer fools, and that she would always champion the cause of the underdog. She told me about Grandma's kindness and her gentle strength, and mostly she would just stroke my hands and tell me that my hands were the same as my grandma's and that we both had the same heart. The closeness I feel to the grandmother I never knew is because my mother chose to remember, and it was through her memories that my Grandma's life was able to touch and inspire mine.

one of the greatest uses of our influence will be to leave a legacy that inspires the generations…

The power of a life does not have to end with that life and the power of a moment does not have to end with that moment. While ever there are women who are willing to take the time to pause and reflect and to tell the stories, then the power of those great lives and those great moments will live on to encourage, inspire, and bring strength for generations to come.

Esther 9:32 is the last we hear about Esther's life and her achievements. She doesn't feature at all in the final chapter of the book. But it is no surprise to me that Esther's final act was to use the full power of her influence to ensure the generations to come would never cease from remembering the faithfulness of God. And it is because of her influence that from the time of ancient Persia and through to this very day Jewish people all around the globe still come together to commemorate and to celebrate the greatness of the God who delivered them.

Each one of us will leave a legacy, an imprint of ourselves upon the earth we inhabited. The question is: 'What kind of legacy will we leave?' *Princess, one of the greatest uses of our influence will be to leave a legacy that inspires the generations to come to know the truth about the God in whose image they have been created.*

[9] Esther 3:7

'Esther had not made known her nationality or her kindred, for Mordecai had charged her not to do so.'

Esther 2:10

ALIGNMENT

There is no greater force on earth than the harmonious alignment of a man and a woman because it is in the unified stand of a male and female that we are most like God.

Man, both male and female, is a reflection of who God is and so it is together that we form our most complete likeness of Him, and it doesn't matter what form that male and female union takes. The life of Esther demonstrates this so effectively. By choosing to align herself first with her adopted parent Mordecai, then with the eunuchs placed over her in the harem, and finally with King Xerxes, her husband and the ruler of her nation, Esther releases the blessing and the favour of God. By bringing herself into alignment with God's word Esther enables His miracle-working power to be released to accomplish the impossible and to bring salvation to His people.

Alignment is the theme that is emphasised most strongly in the book of Esther. The Bible is a book in which no word is wasted, and in the book of Esther in which there are only ten short chapters, so much of it is dedicated to discussing this issue. It is interesting to me that Esther has become so famously known for her beauty, yet her beauty and her physical appearance are mentioned only once. Instead it is her obedience, honour and respect for authority that are mentioned over and over again.

It was alignment, or lack of it, that first created an opportunity for Esther to be raised to her position of influence and authority when Queen Vashti refused to come at the king's command.[10] It was Mordecai's refusal to bow down and show reverence before Haman, that enraged Haman and tipped his hatred of the Jewish people over the edge so that he sought their complete annihilation.

'And when Haman saw that Mordecai did not bow or show him reverence, he was very angry. But he scorned laying hands only on Mordecai. So since they told him Mordecai's nationality, Haman sought to destroy all the Jews.' Esther 3:5-6

Esther, on the other hand, was consistently obedient to the instructions of her caregiver Mordecai both before and after she entered the palace. Once inside the palace Esther found favour and was quickly promoted because of the respect she showed to the eunuchs in charge by following their instructions to the letter.[11]

For Esther, as soon as she entered the palace, everything stopped being about her beauty and instead became all about her obedience and courage. As many as 400 women were brought to the palace in the king's quest to find a wife. Each one of these women was traffic-stopping gorgeous, so once they were inside the palace their beauty no longer set them apart.

The qualities that were the making of Esther were the sweet spirit and the submitted heart she had developed prior to her arrival. It was these attributes that caused her to find favour among all those whom she encountered, and it was the possession of these qualities above all else that caused her to win the heart of the king. *Princess, I believe the greatest lesson we can learn from Esther's life is the power that comes from surrendering our own will and aligning it completely with God's purpose.*

[10] Esther 1:12

[11] Esther 2:15

PRINCESS

Ness & Ruth

We may not share the same
blood but we are family.

'THEREFORE WHAT GOD HAS
JOINED TOGETHER, LET NOT
MAN SEPARATE.'

Matthew 19:6

'And Haman recounted to them the glory of his riches, the abundance of his ten sons, all the things in which the king had promoted him, and how he had advanced him above the princes and servants of the king. Then Haman added, "…Yet all this benefits me nothing as long as I see Mordecai the Jew sitting at the king's gate."' *Esther 5: 11 - 13*

SHE UNDERSTANDS THE DESIRE OF A MAN'S HEART

You don't need to read Cosmopolitan or Cleo magazine to find out what men want. The word of God makes it clear. First and foremost, what men want, need and desire is respect.

In these verses Haman reveals an interesting truth about the hearts of men. After bragging at length to his family and friends about the abundance of his glory, riches and power, Haman goes onto say, 'Yet none of these things satisfy me every time I see Mordecai the Jew.'[12] In spite of all of the great things that were happening in Haman's life and all of his wildest dreams coming true, it was Mordecai's refusal to stand up and show Haman respect earlier that day that filled his heart with wrath and overrode every other success. You see, there was one thing that Haman desired above all else, and it was the one thing that he was not getting: respect.

Remember that God created us, male and female He created us. He knows us inside and out and even better than we know ourselves. I believe that is why God has been so specific in His instruction to women to respect and honour their husbands. God, more than anyone else, knows what His sons need and what their hearts desire.

In the first chapter of Esther we are told that the king is pleased with his first wife Vashti.[13] He thinks she's beautiful and he is so proud of her that he wants to show her off. But when she refuses to come to him he divorces her and determines to give her royal position to one who is 'better' than she is.[14] The question I immediately began asking was, 'better in what way?' It seemed to me that earlier Vashti had been pleasing to the king in so many ways. Yet if there was one quality that Vashti lacked, it was a desire to show honour and respect, and this was a quality that Esther possessed in abundance.

Remember that God created us, male and female He created us. He knows us inside and out and even better than we know ourselves.

Just like in ancient Persia, we live in a world that desires the beauty and charm that women possess, and so many women pursue these things as if they were gold. However, these are not the attributes that will ultimately elevate us or take us to the place of God's best for our lives. There is another attribute that is of much greater value than these and out of all of the many hundreds of women in the Persian court there was only one woman who possessed it. That attribute is alignment. The alignment of our will freely submitted and brought into line with God's word.

Princess, in order for us to realise our potential, we must recognise that no matter how successful and accomplished we are, just like Queen Vashti we will always fall short of the great purpose God has for us until we make the decision to live in alignment with God's word.

12 Esther 5:13

13 Esther 1:11

14 Esther 1:19

PRINCESS

My Nana Edith

She adored her family and her kitchen
was constantly filled with friends who
came over for cups of tea and to enjoy
some of her legendary baking.

'A PERSON STANDING
ALONE CAN BE
ATTACKED AND DEFEATED,
BUT TWO CAN STAND
BACK TO BACK AND
CONQUER. THREE ARE
EVEN BETTER, FOR A
TRIPLE BRAIDED CORD
IS NOT EASILY BROKEN.'

Ecclesiastes 4:12
New Living Translation

'So the king issued a decree to be 'proclaimed throughout all of his kingdom, extensive as it is (that) all wives will give honour to their husbands high and low' and so… He sent letters to all of the royal provinces, to each in its own script and to every people in their own language, saying that every man should rule in his own house and speak there in the language of his own people. If he had foreign wives, let them learn his language!' *Esther 1:20 & 22*

SHE UNDERSTANDS THE POWER OF SUBMISSION

When I first read these verses in Esther Chapter 1, I laughed out loud. They are filled with so much attitude and angst I immediately thought, what was Xerxes' problem?! But I didn't have to search too hard to find out. He was reacting to the humiliation of having his position as head of state and head of his household publicly challenged by his wife, and because of that challenge foreign wives throughout the empire would be made to pay. They would be made to speak Persian only from then on!

But really, why was there such a strong reaction to such a simple act by the queen? So she said 'No!' What was the big deal? Yet wise men were called, a high level meeting was held and a decree was issued. What a fuss! You would think that one of the God-ordained and irrevocable laws of the universe had been turned upside down and the earth was no longer spinning on its axis. Actually, maybe that was the point. The earth may have still been spinning, but an irrevocable and God-ordained law had certainly been challenged.

When God created the universe He established laws and structures to govern and bring order to His creation, and as the source of all authority God established a chain of command through which His authority has been delegated. The word of God outlines some very clear and specific instructions on these lines of authority and how we are meant to relate to one another as a part of His divinely inspired purpose. One of those instructions is that wives must submit themselves to the authority of their husbands.

It's important for us to be aware of and to align ourselves with these delegated lines of authority because God will not move outside of them. The word of God tells us very clearly that the hand of God is limited and constrained by our decisions in this area. Matthew 13 verses 57 and 58 state that the ability of Jesus to perform miracles in his hometown was cut short because the people there refused to acknowledge His authority.

'And they took offense (that is, they were repelled and hindered from acknowledging His authority, and caused to stumble). But Jesus said to them, 'A prophet is not without honour except in his own country and in his own house.' And He did not do many works of power there, because of their unbelief.' Matthew 13:57-58

The hallmark of Esther's life was submission, showing honour and obedience to those whom God had placed in positions of authority over her. This was something she practised with diligence and consistency and it was this characteristic that enabled the hand of God to move and perform tremendous miracles through her life.

So what does submission mean, and what does it involve? A definition from 1 Peter 3:5 in the Amplified Bible is this, 'to become adapted to and (made) secondary and dependant upon.' As I first read this I remember thinking, 'Come on God, you're killing me. Can't you leave me with at least some remnant of self respect?' But I believe that is actually the whole point. God has to remove all the 'self' out of us so that we can become adapted to and completely dependant upon His purposes.

Submission is not an issue specifically limited to women in marriage. The word of God deals with submission in the context of church, the workplace and government, as well as in the home and in family relationships.[15, 16, 17, 18]

However, the reason submission takes on such special significance within the context of marriage is because through the covenant of marriage two people become one in God's sight. If two people in a marriage commit their lives to serving different missions it causes the marriage to be split right down the middle and it will ultimately tear them apart.

'Therefore a man shall leave his father and his mother and shall become united and cleave to his wife, and they shall become one flesh.' Genesis 2:24

My first real encounter with the concept of submission began as I was preparing for my wedding. I have always admired my parent's marriage. After forty years and five children together they are still great friends and very much in love with each other. So I asked my mum if she would give me a copy of the vows she had spoken to my father on their wedding day. As I skimmed through them I almost choked when I came to the part where the woman promises to 'love, honour and OBEY' her husband. I remember thinking, 'Over my dead body will those words ever come out of my mouth!'

No matter how hard I tried to forget about them I just could not get those vows out of my head. And in the corner of my mind, tucked away in some dark recess covered in dust and cobwebs was a scripture I must have read many years before, it was something along the lines of this, 'Wives, submit yourselves to your husbands.' No, it couldn't possibly be true!

But as I read through my Bible I found the very verse I feared the most.

'Wives be subject to your husbands, subordinate and adapt yourselves to them, as is right and fitting and your proper duty in the Lord.' Colossians 3:18

As I felt the panic rising within me I tried to calm myself with thoughts like, 'That verse is probably just a one off. It was probably just put in there to address an issue that was specific to that particular period of time and culture. It no longer has any relevance so I can just dismiss it.' Isn't that right, God? God?!

But as I read more of God's word I unearthed a whole lot more scripture that confirmed my initial finding. What was I to do? I know that the word of God is living and eternal truth and it has transformed my life. So when I saw those words written plainly before me I had no choice but to accept them.

So, yes in the end I did vow to 'love, honour and obey' my husband, and I even surprised myself by not choking on the words as they left my mouth at the altar. But as the journey of our marriage began I realised that saying those words was actually the easy part. Living them was another matter entirely. One of the things that makes the life of Esther so extraordinary is that she didn't just talk about submission, she actually lived it.

The life of Esther demonstrates very clearly that becoming submitted does not require us to become spineless followers or crowd pleasers. True submission actually requires tremendous inner strength, restraint and an unshakeable knowledge of our own personal authority. Most of all, submission requires complete trust in the God to whom we are all ultimately submitted.

Princess, the topic of submission is not glamorous and it is certainly not popular. But one of the things Esther's life reveals is that through submission comes great strength because submission releases God's blessing and enables His hand to move freely through our lives.

[15] Hebrews 13:17

[16] 1 Peter 2:18, Colossians 3:22-23, Ephesians 6:5-9

[17] Romans 13:1, 1 Peter 2:13

[18] Ephesians 6:1-4, Colossians 3:19-21

PRINCESS

PRINCESS

Susan & Grace

Lovely inside and out.

OH GOD YOU ARE
WONDROUSLY AND
FAMOUSLY GREAT.
WHO CAN FAIL TO
BE IMPRESSED BY YOU.'

Jeremiah 10:6
The Message Bible

PRINCESS

'Then I will go before the king, though it is against the law; and if I perish, I perish.' Esther 4:16

SHE HAS AN ETERNAL PERSPECTIVE

I love this verse. It is a source of such great challenge and inspiration. And it is in this moment of intense discussion with Mordecai where Esther not only catches a glimpse of the greater cause in which she is involved, it is also the moment she surrenders her life completely to that cause.

There is nothing as rewarding as being a part of a team and working together toward a common goal, whether it is in sports, at work, in partnership with our families, or within the context of church, partnering with the vision of our senior pastors to change cities and transform nations.

'There is nothing as rewarding as being a part of a team and working together toward a common goal.'

Whatever the context, the bottom line is that in order for us to be a part of anything at all that is bigger than ourselves, we must allow ourselves to be submitted to the bigger picture and take hold of the life-changing revelation: it's not all about me. Let's face it, there is always so much more going on than what we can see from our own narrow and limited perspective.

I imagine for little Esther growing up as part of an obscure minority group in the Persian capital, a life in the palace would not have even been on her radar let alone a goal in her five year plan. There is no way of knowing what Esther's goals and dreams were, but I'd say it's quite likely they didn't include becoming the spokesperson for a condemned people group and possible martyrdom.

The temptation for Esther to refuse Mordecai's request would have been enormous. From within the protective walls of the palace the cause of her people must have appeared so distant and removed from her. But in accepting Mordecai's request she proved her selflessness and the integrity of her heart. It is so interesting that when Esther is accepted into the throne room the first thing the king does is offer her anything she wants, including wealth and power equal to his own and the opportunity to personally receive so much more than she could have ever wanted or dreamed of.[19]

What a telling moment that was, because in the instant when it could have all become about her, Esther chose to remain steadfast to the goal that had been put before her and pursue the interests of her people. Self-preservation and personal agenda were not an issue for Esther because she had allowed a greater cause to capture her heart and her spirit. Who else could God have entrusted with the mission of saving his people other than a woman who had already demonstrated a willingness to lay down her life for that cause?

God did not work through Esther because she was beautiful. He was able to accomplish His purpose through her life because she had an eternal perspective. We can sometimes wonder why God hasn't chosen us to do great things for Him. *Princess, the truth is that it's only when we catch hold of an eternal perspective and display the same selfless determination to God's cause that we can be entrusted with all that He has for us.*

[19] Esther 5:3

PRINCESS

Blessing & Carmen

Laughter is a universal language.

'THE LORD GIVES THE WORD OF POWER; (AND) THE WOMEN WHO BEAR IT ARE A GREAT HOST'

Psalm 68:11

PRINCESS

'So Mordecai went away and did all that Esther had commanded him.' *Esther 4:17*

ALIGNMENT RELEASES
HER AUTHORITY

I believe this is one of the most significant verses in the whole book of Esther. This is the moment of transition in Esther's journey where the full power of her authority is released and she steps into her destiny. Up until this point Esther has been on the receiving end of the commands and instructions of other people, yet it is here that everything is turned up side down and it is Esther who is now in command. Mordecai does not even question this turn of events. He accepts her authority absolutely and he and all of his people submit themselves to it.

It is such a huge misconception that alignment is a sign of weakness and that it causes us to become powerless. In fact, the opposite is true. Alignment increases our strength and it is one of the most underestimated sources of power we have available to us.

I struggled for a long time to accept the command issued to me in God's word to align myself with the authority of my husband. Finally, one day God showed me a vision. In that vision I saw my husband Andrew and I yoked together like two oxen pulling a heavy load. I could see Andrew trying to move the load forward with all of his might. I saw the furrow in his brow and the perspiration dripping down the side of his face. And as the vision panned back I saw from his stance that he was straining forward with everything in him, struggling to pull the load we were both bound to. I could also see myself. But instead of standing up and straining forward, I was sitting down, causing the yoke to become lopsided and uneven. I could see that although I was just sitting there, not running away or trying to pull in the opposite direction, I had actually become a dead weight. Not only was I not helping my husband to move the load we were both yoked to, I was also adding to that load.

'Then the king said to her, What will you have Queen Esther? What is your request? It shall be given you, even to the half of the kingdom.' Esther 5:3

The vision God showed me was such a clear picture of the impact my attitude was having on my husband and our marriage, and also on the call God had placed on both of our lives. Instead of being the strength, help, and the support my husband needed I saw very clearly that I had become a dead weight that was increasing his burden.

That was a defining moment in my life. Right then I made the decision to stand up, to physically demonstrate the decision I was making to accept my husband's authority and to partner with him in the dream God had called us both to. It was not a decision I made lightly because I was aware it would cost me everything, but at the same time it was also a decision that caused me to receive so much more than I ever thought possible because God was able to release in me dreams and potential I never knew I had.

As I reflected on the vision, I realised that Andrew and I were standing alongside each other, equally yoked in every way. I wasn't made to stand ten paces behind him; the yoke would only ever work if I was standing at his side, and I wasn't given a smaller 'girl-sized' portion of the load to carry. Our burden and our responsibility to carry it were exactly the same. What I was required to do was to stand up in the alignment of the yoke God had placed us both in and to start moving forward.

Esther 5 verse 3 contains an amazing truth about alignment and reveals the extent of its power because it is here that the king comes to view Esther as his equal in every way. By extending to Esther an offer of half of his kingdom, Xerxes elevates her to a position of wealth, status and authority equivalent to his own. Now that is powerful!

Regardless of where we stand in the order God has ordained we are all completely equal. And we must never see ourselves in any other way. However, we must choose to bring ourselves into alignment with that order to enable God's full blessing to be released.

The mandate God has placed upon the lives of both His sons and His daughters is exactly the same: 'to have dominion over all of the earth and to go out and subdue it in the service of God and of man.'[20] We were never given dominion over each other but God's word does outline a clear plan within which we are all called to function. Regardless of gender, whether male or female, we will never be able to come into the fullness of the authority God has always intended for us until we first make the choice to align ourselves completely with His word.

'Incredible purpose is not the destiny of a select few, it lies in the pathway of whomever chooses to align themselves with God's word.'

The wonderful and extraordinary power of alignment is demonstrated spectacularly in Esther's life as she works in unison with both Mordecai and Xerxes to achieve the impossible, reverse an irrevocable decree, and bring salvation to a nation of condemned people. *Princess, every human life has the potential for greatness. Incredible purpose is not the destiny of a select few, it lies in the pathway of whomever chooses to align themselves with God's word.*

[20] Genesis 1:28

PRINCESS

'On that day King Xerxes gave the house of Haman, the Jew's enemy, to Queen Esther. And Mordecai came before the king, for Esther had told him what he was to her. And the king took off his signet ring, which he had taken from Haman, and gave it to Mordecai. And Esther appointed Mordecai over the house of Haman.' Esther 8:1-2

PRINCESS

AUTHORITY

The realisation and outworking of our authority is a journey we all must take and it is this destination that God desires each one of us to arrive at. From the moment of our creation it has always been God's intention for us to live and walk in authority. Dominion over all the earth and everything it contains was the gift and the responsibility that God bestowed upon man, both male and female, and God placed this authority within a context: the service of God and of our fellow man.[21]

In the story of Esther we are able to catch a glimpse of what this authority looks like and the extent of its awesome power as Esther is elevated in authority throughout the Persian Empire and makes use of this authority to serve her people and bring honour and glory to God.

One of the keys Esther's life reveals is that the authority we have as women will never come from trying to imitate masculine power. Regardless of gifting or personality type, female authority will always be expressed in a manner that is uniquely feminine. One of the things I love about Esther is that she was, and remained, beautiful, dignified and gracious, yet she also knew how to step out in courage and in faith, and how to stand up and fight for the cause for which she was born.

[21] Genesis 1:28

PRINCESS

Princess Fiona

From the moment we
met I knew that we
would be great friends.

'THE BEST AND MOST BEAUTIFUL THINGS IN THE WORLD CANNOT BE SEEN OR EVEN TOUCHED. THEY MUST BE FELT WITH THE HEART'.

Helen Adams Keller

'If it seems good to the king, let the king and Haman come this day to the dinner that I have prepared for the king.' Esther 5: 4

SHE UNDERSTANDS THE POWER OF PREPARATION

Esther's decision to enter the inner court of Xerxes' throne room uninvited may have been risky but she certainly didn't take any risks when it came to her own preparations or in the way she approached her mission. She had a strategy, she was prepared and she possessed the discipline and the sense of purpose required to execute her plan with confidence and precision.

I love a good plan. I like to know what I'm aiming for and exactly how I'm going to get there. For me nothing compares to the peace and the calm I feel when I get everything out of my head and written down on a piece of paper where it can be ordered and prioritised. Maybe you don't possess the same 'type A' personality as I do, but there is still wisdom and great value to be gained from some strategy and preparation.

From the moment Esther got on board with 'Operation Deliverance of the Jews' she immersed herself in the development of her plan, and the very first thing she did to prepare herself was to pray and seek the counsel of God. The most successful plans will always have the wisdom of heaven as their foundation and this is what underpinned every detail of Esther's strategy. So when it came down to it, how could she fail?

Just like in ancient Persia the battles that we fight today are not against flesh and blood but against the rulers and the powers of evil in the heavenly realms, and so our victories will always be won first in the spirit. However, we so often play a vital role in the answer to the prayers we pray and even though Esther spent three days in prayer and fasting, she still had to roll up her sleeves and get to work. Prayer may be the most crucial form of preparation we can undertake but it does not remove our responsibility to get out of our comfort zones, put our time and money where our prayers are, and get stuck into some hard work.

'For we do not wrestle against flesh and blood, but against the rulers of the darkness of this age, against spiritual hosts of wickedness in the heavenly places.'
Ephesians 6:12 (New King James Version)

When Esther first entered the presence of the king, she didn't just take a deep breath and go for it. In accordance with her plan she had prepared a magnificent feast for the king to enjoy, and when she dressed she placed on her 'royal robes' and presented herself to him in a way that would show him honour and gain her the respect that she needed.[22] And even though her cause was desperate and urgent she didn't just rush in and pre-empt God's timing by blurting everything out too soon. Instead, Esther was able to remain steadfast to her God-given strategy because she had first taken the time to discipline her emotions and carefully prepare her words.

One of the greatest obstacles to our preparation can be unbelief. If we don't believe there is any possibility of our dreams being fulfilled then what is the point in preparing for them? Imagine if Esther had entered the presence of the king without first preparing because she believed with certainty that she was walking to her death. The favour of the king would have been wasted and she would have closed the door on the power of the miraculous working through her life. Her audience with the king would have become just another missed opportunity. It frightens me to think about the number of times I have not even prayed, let alone prepared, because in my heart I have given up before I started, and in my mind I have reduced God to the size of my circumstances and understanding.

Preparation is a statement of faith, and the adoptions of our two sons, first Samuel and then Jonathan three years later, were both occasions where I had to choose to prepare my heart and my life for a dream that required all of my faith, even though making those preparations went against all logic and worldly wisdom.

In New Zealand when a child is placed for adoption, there is a minimum 'cooling off' period of ten days after the baby's birth before any paperwork can be signed. As potential adoptive parents, Andrew and I were strongly advised not to have any contact with our sons during this time, because it very often happens that birth families will change their minds, and so we would just be exposing ourselves to unnecessary pain and disappointment.

We could certainly see the wisdom in this advice, especially when it came from the mouth of a kind social worker who had seen so many hearts broken before us. It was, however, advice we could not afford to follow because we had received a promise from God, and we believed that Samuel and Jonathan were the fulfillment of His promise.

Like any parents, our desire to bond with and care for our children was greater than our desire to protect our hearts, no matter how foolhardy it may have seemed to the people around us. So, as soon as we could we started our preparations. We bought baby clothes, cots and nappies, we organised the nursery and from the day of our children's births, we were there. Andrew and I worked in shifts to care for our babies for the duration of their time in hospital and foster care. The darkest moments of my life so far were when in each of the adoptions, just days before the signing of the final documents, we were told that the birth families had changed their minds and that we could have no more contact with the children we had thought were ours.

The one thing that tormented me most during those dark days was that I didn't even know what to pray. I hadn't given birth to our babies, we had no legal right to them and the last thing we ever wanted to do was steal someone's child. In spite of our confusion Andrew and I had to make a choice, either give up and let our dreams die, or persist in spite of the pain of allowing our hope to continue.

Andrew and I choose to persist and to pray. Our prayer was simply this, 'God please give the birth family peace whatever their final decision.' During that time God did what only He can. He worked miracles. On both occasions, only days after hearing that the door was firmly closed with no hope for change, everything was turned around and that same door was suddenly flung wide open. At the signing of the final paperwork for both Samuel and then Jonathan, the birth families of each of our boys said the same thing: they had never felt such peace about a decision before in their lives.

… do what we can, and step out in faith and prepare…

I am so grateful that I put my heart on the line and prepared myself to be the mother of my children, because when they finally came home I already knew them. I had been with them since their births, I knew their routines, I knew their cries and the quirks in their personalities; and they knew me, they knew my touch, my smell and they knew my voice. From the moment they arrived home we didn't miss a beat.

Our God is a miracle-working God who will deliver on each one of His promises and do what only He can. But He also asks the same of us, that we do what we can, step out in faith and prepare. *Princess, it is with faith-filled preparation that the full potential of our authority will be realised.*

22 Esther 5:1 & 4

My Hero
Anne with my son Samuel

Her passion for God and love for
people has inspired my life.

'FOR THE EYES OF THE LORD MOVE
TO AND FRO THROUGHOUT
THE WHOLE EARTH THAT HE MAY
STRONGLY SUPPORT THOSE WHOSE
HEARTS ARE COMPLETELY HIS'

2 Chronicles 16:9
New American Standard Bible

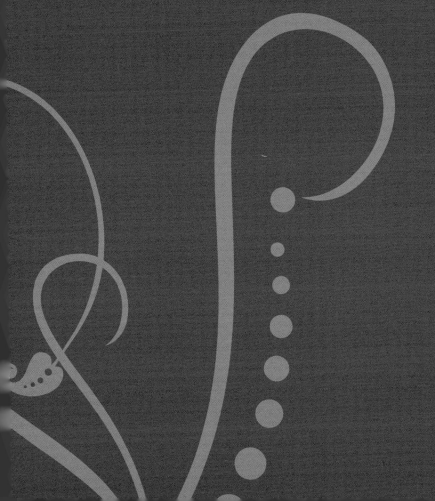

'And in every province and in every city, wherever the king's command and his decree came, the Jews had gladness and joy, a feast and a holiday.' *Esther 8:17*

SHE UNDERSTANDS THE
POWER OF A CELEBRATION

I find this verse completely fascinating and it is such a huge key to developing perseverance and renewing our strength. What I find most interesting about this verse is that this joyful feast and celebration actually occur before any lasting victory had been experienced by the Jews. The king may have issued a decree allowing the Jewish people to defend themselves against attack, but the impossibility of their situation still remained because they were a minority, a remnant of people bought back to Persia as captives of war many years earlier. This tiny remnant was not even a cohesive group united together in one place. We are told that the Jews were 'scattered' and 'dispersed' throughout the vast empire. What chance did this scattered remnant have against the whole Persian army?

'There is a certain people scattered abroad and dispersed among the peoples in all the provinces of your kingdom; their laws are different from every other people.'
Esther 3:8

And yet, with just a few months remaining before the date set for their annihilation, and in the midst of the impossibility and continuing desperation of their circumstances, what did the Jewish people do? They celebrated, feasted, rejoiced and declared a holiday.

On first reading I thought the stress of it all must have gotten to the Jews and made them go a bit crazy. Wouldn't their time have been better spent sharpening their swords and working on their military strategy?

As we have seen there is wisdom in preparation, but something the Jewish people also realised was the great value that came from having their spirits lifted and their strength renewed. Even in the tough times, the journey of our lives is made so much more enjoyable when it is punctuated with times of celebration.

I love to run. It is one of my most favourite things in the world to do. I love to get outside in the fresh air and stretch my legs and run for as long as my husband will agree to look after the children. When I'm running I feel free. It's when I'm running that I do my best thinking and see with the greatest clarity, and it is when I'm running that I feel closest to God.

A couple of years ago I ran a marathon. The course was set around a (very big!) lake which was surrounded by rainforest, and for the most part the scenery was stunning. So you would think given the beauty of my surroundings and my love for running I would have been in my absolute element throughout the race. This was not the case. Despite my passion for running, completing that marathon was hard work. A marathon is a long way! The course may have been beautiful but it was also mountainous and it rained torrentially for the duration of the race, and running down steep hills through slippery mud just kills your feet and legs. I wasn't far into the race when I was already in a great deal of pain.

Sometimes the trials of life can take you by surprise and even when you are in God's will and doing something you really love there will be times when it is just hard work and even painful. The biggest lesson I learned in running that marathon was the power of some simple encouragement.

Strategically placed throughout the race were drink stations, where as you ran by you could grab a cup of water or an energy drink. However, it was not the drinks but the people handing them out who were really the ones who refreshed and sustained us. As well as handing out drinks they also gave out encouragement with great generosity. These complete strangers clapped and cheered us on, applauding how far we had already come and reminding us of our goal, the finish line.

The most difficult part of that race was the halfway point. After running so far already, I knew that the end was still nowhere in sight and that I still had such a long way to go. But the halfway point drink station was where they pulled out all of the stops. At this station they were having a party, singing silly songs and wearing even sillier hats, and every runner who passed by got showered with confetti and streamers and received an ovation.

Completing a marathon is as much about mental endurance as physical strength, and my race strategy soon became centered around those drink stations. 'You can do it, just make it to the next drink station.' It was at that next station where I received the encouragement and the motivation I needed to keep pushing through to the next station, and the next, until the finish line was finally in sight.

A marathon is such a great metaphor for life, and in the same way as the refreshing and encouragement I received at those drink stations helped me to complete my race, setting time aside to celebrate the victories already won and to affirm and encourage each other will enable us to persevere and push through, even in the hard times.

So often when things get tough, when our worlds start to fall apart around us, or when we are facing those mountains that seem impossible to move, we choose to withdraw and isolate ourselves. But these are actually the very moments when we need the support and encouragement that comes from standing together and combining our faith with the faith of our friends. The word of God puts it like this, 'A person standing alone can be attacked and defeated, but two can stand back to back and conquer. Three are even better, for a triple-braided cord is not easily broken.'[23]

The reason the Jewish people were able to celebrate and claim their victory in spite of their circumstances was because they knew the sovereignty of the God they served. They may have still had a long way to go and some big battles to fight, but they knew that if their God could change the heart of a king, and if He could overthrow an evil tyrant and replace him with a God-fearing and righteous man, then their God could save them. There was nothing that He could not do.

'So Mordecai went forth from the presence of the king in royal apparel of blue and white, with a great crown of gold and with a robe of fine linen and purple; and the city of Sushan shouted and rejoiced. The Jews had light (a dawn of new hope) and gladness, and joy and honour.'
Esther 8:15-16

So, to prepare themselves for the greatest battle of their lives the Jewish people chose to take some time out to encourage each other and to celebrate the faithfulness of God.

Princess, with all we are juggling amidst the craziness of life, pausing for a moment to celebrate and to remind ourselves of the greatness of God will not only refresh and strengthen us, it will also prevent worry and anxiety from blinding us to our authority and the victory we will always have in God.

23 Ecclesiastes 4:12

PRINCESS

My mother-in-law
Margaret

Mother of 8, mother-in-law of 6, grandmother
of 15, yet she has a way of making us
all feel like we are the favourite.

'SHE IS FAR MORE PRECIOUS THAN JEWELS AND HER VALUE IS FAR ABOVE RUBIES AND PEARLS.'

Proverbs 31:10

And the king said to Esther the queen, 'The Jews have slain and destroyed 500 men in Sushan, the capital, and the ten sons of Haman. What then have they done in the provinces?! Now what is your petition? It shall be granted to you. What is your request further? It shall be done.' Then Esther said, 'If it pleases the king, … let the dead bodies of Haman's sons be hanged on the gallows.' *Esther 9: 12-13*

SHE HAS THE POWER
OF ENDURANCE

I wonder if Esther knew when she signed up for the job of saving her people that it would turn out to be such bloodthirsty work? At Esther's command the Jewish people killed over 75,000 people. It takes some big shoulders to bear that kind of responsibility.

'And the other Jews who were in the king's provinces gathered together to defend their lives, had relief and rest from their enemies and slew them who hated them, seventy- five thousand; but on the spoil they laid not their hands.' Esther 9:16

We all like the thought of having authority and of wielding it to overcome our enemies, but when it actually comes down to the point of getting our hands dirty and engaging in warfare, the use of our authority often becomes much less attractive. An even greater challenge still is the decision to stand up and accept responsibility for the outcome of that battle, no matter how great the carnage.

When I was a little girl learning Bible stories in Sunday school I remember thinking that Esther was a bit of a lightweight.

She was a beauty queen so she must have been an airhead, right? Instead, I admired women like Abigail for her wisdom and use of strategy, and Jael because you just have to love a woman who has the nerve and wherewithal to drive a tent peg through the temple of her enemy as he innocently slept inside her tent.

However, I've since come to the conclusion that Esther takes the prize for being, 'the gutsiest woman in the Bible'. She refused to allow herself to be overwhelmed by the size of the task at hand, or to shrink back from any part of it even though it involved hard and dirty work that would leave her with blood on her hands.

An insightful attribute of Esther's use of her authority was that she was determined to use every opportunity it gave her to see her mission through to its completion. Esther was not satisfied that all of the enemies of the Jews, including the entire household of Haman, had been killed.[24] She took things one step further by ensuring the corpses of Haman's ten sons were put on public display and hanged from the gallows, to publicly declare that the house of Haman had been completely annihilated once and for all.

If we look more closely into the genealogy of Haman we see that he is the son of Hammadetha the Agagite and a direct descendant of Agag the Amalekite king.[25] Agag was a sworn enemy of the Jewish people and hundreds of years earlier God had entrusted King Saul with the task of destroying Agag and wiping the Amalekites off the face of the earth.

King Saul started out so well, destroying all of the Amalekites by the sword as God had commanded him,[26] but it was his decisions at the end of the battle that were his downfall. At Saul's instruction the life of Agag the king was spared, and instead of destroying all the livestock as God had commanded him, Saul chose to keep 'everything that was good'[27] for himself.

'Behold, to obey is better than sacrifice,…
For rebellion is as the sin of witchcraft, And
stubbornness is as iniquity and idolatry.
Because you have rejected the word of the
Lord, He also has rejected you from being king.'
1 Samuel 15:22-23

Saul had come so close to fulfilling God's purpose but in the end he fell short because he was faint hearted and became sidetracked by the plunder and spoils of war. Saul's decision to choose personal gain over obedience was the failing that robbed him of his authority and caused him to forfeit his destiny. His failure to see God's purpose through to its completion caused God to give his royal position to another, a young man named David, and the purpose that God had first intended for Saul was placed into the hands of a young woman from another generation to fulfill. Saul may have been gifted and anointed, but he lacked endurance and God could no longer trust him.

The behaviour of Queen Esther provides an interesting comparison. Under Esther's leadership the Jews smote all their enemies, 'but on the spoil they laid not their hands.' Unlike Saul before her, Esther was not distracted by the rewards of her victory, instead she remained focused on seeing her mission through to its end, no matter how costly and unpleasant it was.

The power of endurance is the hallmark of the life of my mother-in-law, Margaret. To begin with, she is the mother of eight children. In my opinion, that fact alone is enough to qualify her as an endurance superhero. But what really sets her apart was her commitment and perseverance throughout my husband's illness as a teenager.

When Andrew was 13 years old he was diagnosed with an aggressive form of leukemia. When all of the normal treatments failed, the only hope doctors could offer Andrew was an experimental form of chemotherapy and a bone marrow transplant. The chemotherapy was delivered straight into Andrew's brain via a small golf ball-sized shunt inserted into his skull, and from the moment it was injected Andrew would scream in agony as it immediately caused a spinal migraine, loss of all muscle control and paralysis of his limbs which lasted for hours. This cruel treatment was to be administered every week for a year, but after six weeks Andrew suffered a nervous breakdown and the treatment was stopped.

Andrew was adamant that he would prefer death to the ongoing treatment.

The doctor's advice was that unless Andrew continued the treatment, he would certainly die and if he persisted, his chance of survival would increase to 10%. Even the greatest optimist would have to admit these were not good odds. But Andrew's parents refused to give up on their son's life, and with their encouragement Andrew decided to push through. The treatments re-commenced but this time Andrew also received a memory loss drug, which meant that although he would experience all of the same pain he would not be able to remember it the next day.

For a year, Margaret sat by Andrew's side and held his hand while he went through torturous treatment after torturous treatment. As a mother, I cannot imagine what it would have been like for her to sit at the side of her baby boy while he endured such agony. If it were me I would have insisted on having my own supply of memory loss drugs.

But Margaret pushed through and persevered because she had made the decision to fix her eyes on the 10% chance that Andrew would make it and not the 90% chance that he wouldn't. Drawing on all of her strength and determination she encouraged Andrew and kept his eyes on the finish line until the treatment was completed and the cancer was gone.

Andrew's recovery was, in the eyes of the medical profession, 'miraculous', and his performance throughout his chemotherapy and transplant became a benchmark for cancer treatment throughout the world. But his recovery came at an enormous cost to the woman who encouraged and comforted him through it, and I cannot watch my husband playing with our two boys without thanking God for my mother-in-law and what she endured to bring that beautiful family scene into being.

God created Eve to bring completion to Adam, and in the same way He also raised up Esther to bring completion to His purpose. *Princess, as women we have been given the power of endurance and one of the most important features of our authority is perseverance and the ability to bring completion.*

24 Esther 9:13

25 Esther 3: 1

26 1 Samuel 15:3

27 1 Samuel 15:9

My nieces
Courtney & Sophia

The journey continues...

'I HEARD THE VOICE
OF THE LORD, SAYING, 'WHOM
SHALL I SEND? AND WHO
WILL GO FOR US? THEN SAID
I, HERE I AM; SEND ME'

Isaiah 6:8

PRINCESS

'If Mordecai, before whom you have begun to fall, is of the offspring of the Jews, you cannot prevail against him, but shall surely fall before him' *Esther 6:13*

SHE KNOWS THE POWER
OF HER GOD

This is such a powerful verse because in it, Haman's wife Zeresh has identified an eternal truth. It is impossible to stand against the one true God and prevail. It will always be a losing battle. God is the source of all authority and there is no authority in either the heavens or on earth that can overcome Him. His purpose will always be sovereign. All that remains for us to do is to align ourselves with that purpose and in faith begin to walk it out, knowing that the authority of heaven underpins our every step.

Esther's initial response to Mordecai, that his request is both impossible and suicidal, demonstrates what happens when we focus on what we know in our heads and not who we know in our hearts. When Esther set her focus on the authority of men, she was paralysed and incapable of seeing beyond her circumstances.

'All the king's servants and the people of the king's provinces know that any person, be it man or woman, who shall go into the inner court to the king, without being called, shall be put to death; there is but one law.' Esther 4:11

It was only after Mordecai informed Esther that relief and deliverance would arise for the Jews whether she chose to be a part of it or not that Esther was reminded of the sovereignty of God and she was able to see beyond the fear of man.[28]

We all remember that poignant scene where Esther puts on her royal robes and enters the inner courts of the king's throne room uninvited and we hold our breath as we anticipate the king's response. Will he hold out his golden scepter and in doing so spare her life? Or, will she perish?

This is when the authority that comes from knowing who you really are kicks in. When Esther entered that throne room, not knowing if each step would be her last, she did so without cowering or flinching and she boldly stood before the greatest kingdom on earth because she knew the authority of the Kingdom she represented.

Even though Persian law clearly stated that any person who entered the king's inner court without first being summoned would be put to death, Esther had come to realise there was an authority even greater than any earthly law at work and it was in this authority that she had learned to place her trust. On every occasion that Esther entered Xerxes' presence, his response to her was always the same, 'What is your petition Queen Esther? It shall be granted to you. And what is your request? It shall be performed.' Whenever Esther stood in the presence of the king, time and time again, he extended to her unprecedented favour and authority equal to his own.

Something the life of Esther makes very clear is that once the authority of God has been established in our lives, it is enduring, and the authority He bestows cannot be removed by men. It was this revelation that was the source of Esther's courage, and placing her life in God's hands was a carefully considered choice.

'the authority He bestows cannot be removed by men.'

Some time ago I was on the receiving end of some bad service from our bank. Some errors had occurred in our accounts and it seemed that no one at the bank had any interest in resolving or correcting the problems. Now if there is one thing that makes me lose my cool, it's bad service. Just the thought of it gets my heart racing. I cannot just sit back and allow it to happen, I have to say and do something.

My natural instincts are always to play by the rules and so, in the first instance, I chose to follow the bank's standard grievance handling procedure. But let me tell you, that grievance handling procedure brought me nothing but grief and complete frustration. Every person I spoke with had the same response, 'I'm sorry I don't have the authority to give you that information,' 'I'm sorry I don't have the authority to make that change,' 'I'm sorry, I can't help you, I don't have the authority.' It got to the point where if I had heard the words 'no authority' one more time, I would have screamed!

I knew my only hope for a breakthrough was to find someone in that bank who had some authority. So I went online and found out the name of the bank's General Manager. I then sent him an email outlining all of my frustrations and my expectations for them to be resolved. I sent that email at 9.30pm one evening. At 7.30am the very next morning I received a phone call at home. It was the General Manager calling to personally apologise for all of the problems I had experienced and to assure me that each one of those problems would be corrected to my satisfaction by 9.00am that morning. After two weeks of frustration, red tape and no change, the moment I went to the place of authority, Ka-Boom! An immediate response, effective and lasting change, and the impenetrable walls of bureaucracy and procedure came tumbling down.

I remember the walk I took a few years ago from my house to the house of my neighbour, and how on the surface it appeared to be so minor and insignificant. It was in fact one of the hardest and most worthwhile things I have ever done. That walk was all about stepping away from the place where I had no authority, shutdown by my insecurities and stepping into the place of freedom and authority that comes from obedience to God.

Just like Esther before us, we must choose to go to the place of authority if we want to get things done. While ever we choose to live in the places where we have no authority, consumed by our fears and inadequacies, then we will remain paralysed, the journey of our lives continually obstructed and robbed of purpose.

'And no man could withstand them, for the fear of them had fallen upon on all the peoples. And all the princes of the provinces, and the chief rulers, and the governors, and they who attended to the king's business, helped the Jews because the fear of Mordecai had fallen upon them.' Esther 9:2-3

The number and magnitude of miracles that occur in Esther 9 are too numerous to detail. But they serve as a steadfast reminder that nothing is impossible for God and at the end of the day the battle belongs to Him, and He never loses a fight.

Princess, the great benefit that comes from aligning ourselves with God's purpose is that our lives then become conduits for the limitless power of heaven. In the final chapters of Esther's story, we see that when the hand of God moves the power of the miraculous is breathtaking to behold, no obstacle is left standing, and nothing is impossible!

28 Esther 4:14

'Haman, son of Hammedatha, the Agagite, the enemy of all the Jews, had plotted against the Jews to destroy them...But when Esther bought the matter before the king, he commanded in writing that Haman's wicked scheme which he had devised against the Jews should return upon his own head, and that he and his sons should be hanged on the gallows.' Esther 9:24-25

THE CALL

The book of Esther is not just the story of a beautiful girl. It is a demonstration of the sovereignty of God revealed through the life of a woman. It is also the fulfillment of God's original intention for mankind outlined in Genesis 1, as Esther first aligns herself with God's purpose, then steps into her authority, and surrenders her life to the cause of serving her God and her people.

Like Esther, we live in a world where there are no human solutions to the great needs that face our planet. Just as the course of events that unfolded to bring victory to the Jewish people in ancient Persia were not natural but supernatural, so it remains that it is only through the power of a supernatural God that the justice and the transformation our earth is crying out for can be delivered. God's method for delivering that supernatural power has not changed. He is looking for men and women who will be His hands and His feet.

I believe God is calling women across the earth to rise up and to embrace their feminine identity; to take their place alongside men; and to align themselves with the eternal purpose of making God's name great throughout the earth.

In Esther 4:14, Mordecai reminds Esther that God's plan will be sovereign regardless of whether she chooses to become involved or not. The choice Esther is then left to consider is this, to either become a part of the plan for the salvation of God's people or to step aside and allow God to raise up someone else in her place.

So Princess, now that you know who you are, will you embrace the same courageous choice as Esther and become a part of the rescue team, or will you choose to do nothing and become a damsel in distress awaiting rescue?